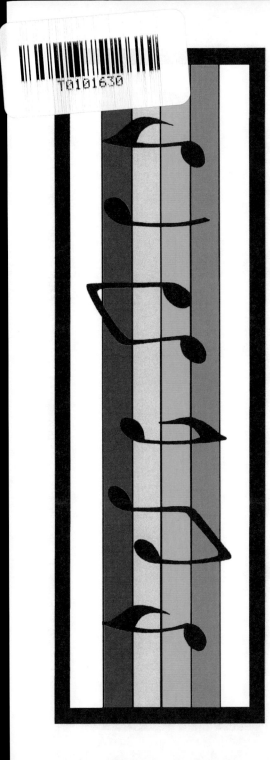

Certificate of Participation

Issued to

_____

for

_____

Date _____

Teacher _____

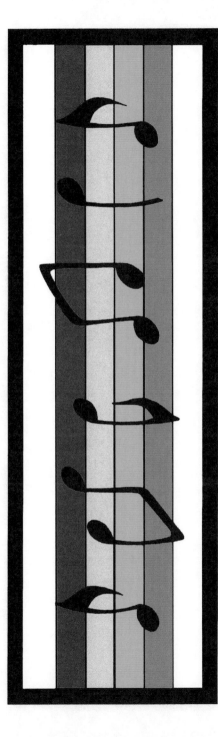

Certificate of Participation

Issued to

_____

for

_____

Date

Teacher

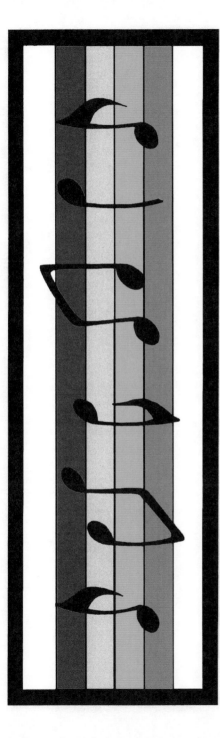

Certificate of Participation

Issued to

_____

for

_____

_____
Date

_____
Teacher

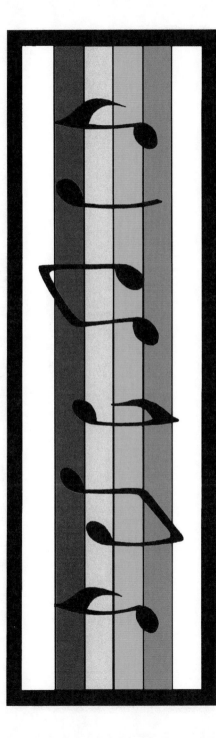

Certificate of Participation

Issued to

_____

for

_____

Date _____

Teacher

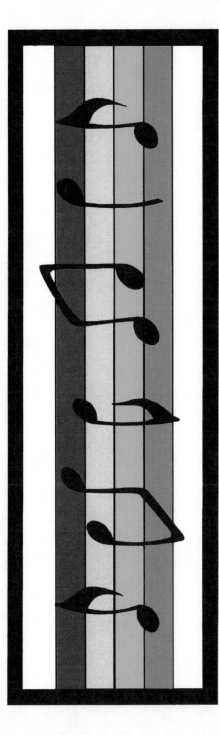

Certificate of Participation

Issued to

_____

for

_____

Date _____

Teacher

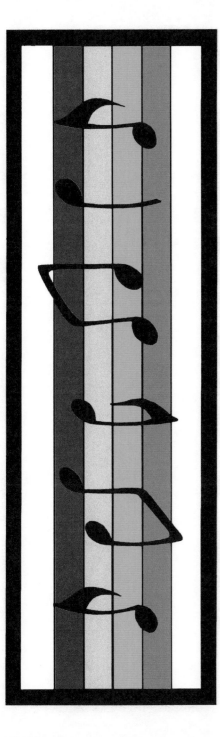

Certificate of Participation

Issued to

_____

for

_____

_____
Date

_____
Teacher

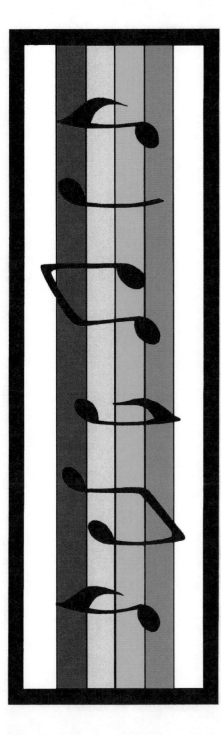

Certificate of Participation

Issued to

_____

for

_____

_____

Date

_____

Teacher

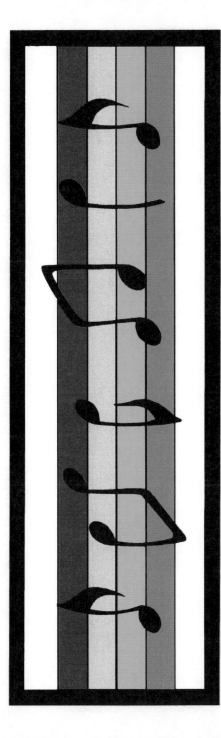

Certificate of Participation

Issued to

_____

for

_____

_____
Date

_____
Teacher

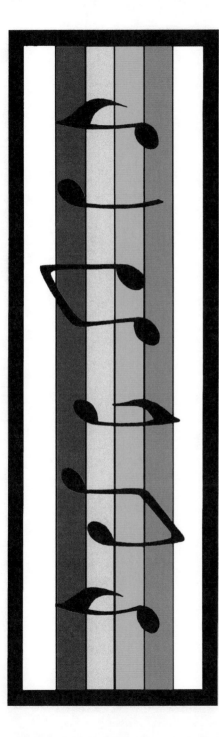

Certificate of Participation

Issued to

_____

for

_____

Date _____

Teacher

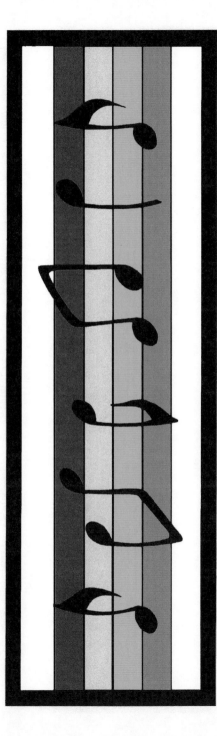

Certificate of Participation

Issued to

_____

for

_____

_____
Date

_____
Teacher

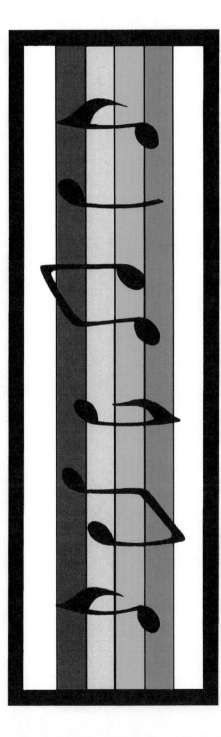

Certificate of Participation

Issued to

_____

for

_____

Date _____

Teacher _____

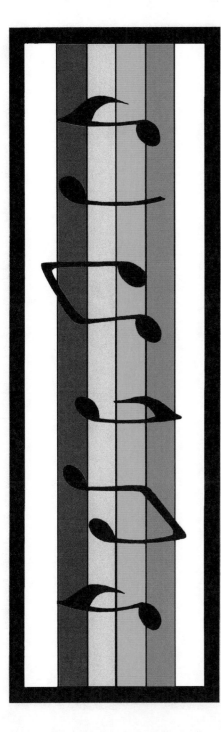

Certificate of Participation

Issued to

_____

for

_____

Date _____

_____

Teacher